A Guide to Mental Health and Healing

Strategies for a Happier Life

PUBLISHED BY — SAJID NASEEM

Contents

Introduction

In today's fast-paced world, mental health has become an essential part of overall well-being. As we navigate life's complexities while balancing work, relationships, and personal aspirations, many of us face challenges that can significantly impact our mental and emotional health. Mental health issues are often shrouded in stigma and misunderstanding, yet they are increasingly recognized as having a profound impact on individuals and society as a whole. This book aims to shed light on the multifaceted nature of mental health and provide practical ideas and strategies for people who want to improve their well-being and overcome the invisible challenges they may face.

Chapter 1, Understanding Mental Health, builds the foundation by exploring what mental health actually means and covering emotional, psychological, and social well-being. It highlights the importance of mental health in how we think, feel, and behave, and addresses the spectrum of mental health from thriving to struggling.

Chapter 2, The Invisible Struggle — Recognizing the Signs, digs into the complexity of mental health problems. This chapter provides important tools for identifying signs of mental health issues, emphasizing that early recognition is key to effective intervention and support.

Chapter 3, The Power of Therapy — Professional Help and Its Impact, describes the different therapeutic approaches available and how professional help can be a transformative force on your path to healing. This chapter demystifies therapy and focuses on its role in promoting personal growth, resilience, and emotional regulation.

Chapter 4, Mindfulness and Meditation — Tools for Everyday Mental Health, explores mindfulness practice and meditation as accessible tools for managing stress, anxiety, and overthinking. The chapter offers practical ways to incorporate mindfulness into everyday life, helping readers cultivate presence even amid life's challenges.

Chapter 5, The Role of Lifestyle — Exercise, Sleep, and Nutrition, examines the significant impact lifestyle can have on mental health. It highlights the importance of physical health, including regular exercise, adequate sleep, and a balanced diet, as the foundation for optimal mental health.

Chapter 6, Building Resilience — Coping Strategies and Emotional Strength, offers insights into developing resilience and effective coping strategies. This chapter emphasizes the importance of emotional strength in coping with adversity and promotes a proactive approach to mental health.

Chapter 7, Social Media, Technology, and Mental Health, explores the complex relationship between technology and mental health. This chapter focuses on the pros and cons of social media and examines its impact on self-esteem, anxiety, and social connection in the digital age.

Chapter 8, The Journey of Healing — Embracing Growth and Change, closes the book by exploring the ongoing process of healing and personal growth. This chapter encourages readers to embrace their own journeys, recognizing that healing is not linear but rather a dynamic and evolving process.

This book is designed to be a compassionate companion for your mental health journey, offering a deeper understanding of mental health complexity alongside practical, evidence-based strategies. Whether you want to understand your own mental health better, support your loved ones, or begin a path toward healing, this book aims to give you the resources and guidance to move forward with confidence. As we navigate the intricacies of mental health together, let us cultivate awareness, resilience, and hope for a better future.

Chapter 1
Understanding Mental Health

Mental health is an integral part of overall well-being. Just as physical health is essential to living a full and satisfying life, mental health plays a key role in how we perceive and interact with the world. Our mental health affects the way we think, feel, and behave, as well as our ability to cope with stress, communicate with others, and make decisions. Yet for many, mental health remains a misunderstood or stigmatized subject, often leading to misunderstanding and a lack of proper care. The importance of mental health has received considerable attention in recent years. People are beginning to understand that mental health is not simply the absence of mental illness but rather a state of mental, emotional, and psychological well-being. As mental health issues become more visible in the public sphere, it is essential that we gain a better understanding of what mental health is, how it differs from mental illness, and the various factors that affect it.

The purpose of this chapter is to introduce the concept of mental health, explain what it means, and clarify the difference between mental health and mental illness. We will explore some of the most common mental health issues, the biological, psychological, and social factors that contribute to mental health, and the stigma and misconceptions surrounding this important aspect of our well-being.

Mental Health vs. Mental Illness

One of the most common misconceptions about mental health is the confusion between mental health and mental illness. Although these terms are often used interchangeably, they refer to different concepts.

- Mental health is a state of well-being in which a person realizes their own potential, can cope with the normal stresses of life, work productively, and make a contribution to their community. It encompasses emotional, psychological, and social well-being.

- A mental illness, on the other hand, refers to a specific, diagnosable disorder that affects mood, thinking, or behaviour. Mental illnesses are health conditions that can affect a person's daily life and may require specialized treatment.

Mental Health as a Continuum

It is important to understand that mental health exists on a continuum, ranging from optimal health to severe mental illness. At one end of the continuum, a person may experience good mental and physical well-being, characterized by emotional resilience, adaptability, and the ability to cope with life's challenges. At the other end, serious mental health problems such as debilitating depression or anxiety can impair a person's functioning.

People move along this continuum at different points in their lives. Mental health is not static, and various factors — such as life events, stress, relationships, and biological predisposition — can influence where a person falls on the continuum at any given time.

Mental Illness: What It Is and What It Is Not

Mental illness refers to conditions that interfere with a person's thinking, feelings, mood, ability to relate to others, and daily functioning. These conditions vary in severity and can be temporary or long-term. Mental illnesses such as depression, anxiety disorders, schizophrenia, and bipolar disorder are real medical conditions that affect a person's brain chemistry and mental health.

Mental health and mental illness are distinct concepts, but they are closely related: just as physical health can be poor without the presence of a chronic illness, mental health can be poor without the presence of a mental illness. Similarly, people with mental illnesses such as depression can maintain good mental health through treatment, support, and self-care. Understanding the difference between mental health and mental illness helps us approach mental health from a more holistic and compassionate perspective. Everyone experiences fluctuations in their mental health, and even people without a formal diagnosis can benefit from paying close attention to their emotional and psychological needs.

Common Mental Health Issues

There are many mental health conditions, and each affects people differently. Some conditions are more common than others, but all mental health issues deserve attention and care. Here we look at some of the most common mental health disorders, including depression, anxiety, and post-traumatic stress disorder (PTSD).

1. Depression

Depression is one of the most common mental health disorders in the world, affecting millions of people each year. More than just feeling sad or going through a tough time, depression is a persistent mood disorder that significantly impacts a person's ability to function in everyday life. Symptoms of depression can include:

- Persistent feelings of sadness, hopelessness, or emptiness

- Loss of interest in activities that were once enjoyable

- Feeling tired or a lack of energy

- Difficulty concentrating or making decisions

- Changes in appetite and sleep patterns

- Thoughts of death or suicide

Depression comes in many forms, including major depressive disorder (MDD), dysthymia (a milder but chronic form of depression), and seasonal affective disorder (SAD), which occurs during certain times of the year — usually winter, when there is less natural light. Depression is often treatable with a combination of medication, therapy, and lifestyle changes, but the stigma surrounding mental illness can prevent people from seeking the help they need.

2. Anxiety Disorders

Anxiety disorders are among the most common mental health problems, characterized by excessive worry, fear, or nervousness that is out of proportion to the situation at hand. While it is natural to feel anxious from time to time, anxiety disorders involve persistent and overwhelming feelings of fear or dread that can interfere with daily life. There are several types of anxiety disorders:

- **Generalized anxiety disorder (GAD):** Characterized by chronic worry about many aspects of life, even when there is little reason to worry.

- **Panic disorder:** Involves sudden, intense panic attacks and may include physical symptoms such as a racing heart, shortness of breath, and dizziness.

- **Social anxiety disorder:** Causes extreme fear of social situations and of being judged or embarrassed in front of others.

- **Phobias:** Intense fear of certain objects or situations, such as heights, spiders, or flying.

Anxiety disorders can have a significant impact on a person's quality of life and can lead to avoidance behaviours, social isolation, and difficulties at work or school. Treatment options such as cognitive behavioural therapy (CBT), exposure therapy, and medication can help individuals manage their symptoms and regain control over their lives.

3. Post-Traumatic Stress Disorder (PTSD)

PTSD is a mental health condition that can develop after experiencing or witnessing a traumatic event, such as a natural disaster, a violent attack, or military combat. Not everyone who is traumatized develops PTSD, but those who do may relive the event through flashbacks, nightmares, and intrusive thoughts. They may also avoid people, places, or situations that remind them of the trauma and experience anxiety and emotional numbness.

Common symptoms of PTSD include:

- Repeated, distressing memories or dreams of the traumatic event

- Avoidance of reminders of the trauma

- Hypervigilance or an exaggerated startle response

- Feelings of detachment or emotional numbness

- Difficulty concentrating or sleeping

PTSD can affect anyone, regardless of age or background, and can significantly impact a person's ability to function in everyday life. Treatment for PTSD often includes trauma-focused therapies, such as Eye Movement Desensitization and Reprocessing (EMDR) and Cognitive Processing Therapy (CPT), which help people process and reduce the emotional impact of trauma.

Biological, Psychological, and Social Factors Influencing Mental Health

Mental health is shaped by a complex interplay of biological, psychological, and social factors. Understanding these factors helps us recognize the many influences on mental health and guides more effective mental health care.

1. Biological Factors

Mental health has a significant biological component, meaning our genetic makeup and brain chemistry play a crucial role in influencing mental well-being.

- **Genetics:** A family history of a mental disorder may increase a person's chances of developing a similar condition. While having a genetic predisposition does not mean someone will necessarily experience a mental disorder, it may increase their vulnerability.

- **Brain chemistry:** Neurotransmitters — chemical messengers in the brain such as serotonin, dopamine, and norepinephrine — play a role in regulating mood, emotions, and behaviour. Imbalances in these neurotransmitters are often associated with mental health disorders such as depression and anxiety.

- **Medical conditions:** Physical health conditions such as chronic pain, hormone imbalances, and neurological disorders can affect mental health. For example, thyroid problems can mimic symptoms of depression, and chronic pain can contribute to anxiety and mood disorders.

- **Substance use:** The use of alcohol, drugs, and other substances can have serious effects on mental health. Substance use disorders can occur alongside mental health disorders, creating a cycle in which one condition worsens the other.

2. Psychological Factors

Psychological factors, such as early life experiences, coping mechanisms, and personality traits, also play a crucial role in mental health.

- **Childhood experiences:** Early life experiences such as trauma, neglect, abuse, and attachment disruption can shape a person's mental health in adulthood.

People who experience adverse events in childhood are more likely to develop mental health disorders, especially if they lack emotional support and healthy coping mechanisms.

- **Cognitive patterns:** The way we think can influence how we feel and behave. People with mental health disorders often struggle with negative thinking patterns, such as catastrophizing, black-and-white thinking, or focusing only on the negative aspects of a situation. These cognitive distortions can lead to anxiety, depression, and low self-esteem.

- **Emotion regulation:** The ability to manage and regulate emotions is essential to mental health. People who have difficulty processing and expressing their emotions may be more prone to mood disorders and anxiety.

- **Personality traits:** Certain personality traits, such as high levels of neuroticism or perfectionism, can predispose individuals to mental health problems. For example, people with perfectionistic tendencies may be more likely to experience anxiety and burnout.

3. Social Factors

Social and environmental factors also play an important role in mental health. These include relationships, living conditions, socioeconomic status, and cultural background.

- **Relationships:** Healthy and supportive relationships are essential for mental well-being. People with strong social connections tend to have better mental health outcomes, while those who live alone or in isolation may be at higher risk of developing mental health problems.

- **Socioeconomic status:** Poverty, unemployment, and financial instability can have a significant impact on mental health. People living in poverty are more likely to experience chronic stress, which can lead to mental health problems such as depression and anxiety.

- **Cultural and environmental influences:** Cultural norms, social expectations, and environmental factors such as access to health care and community support can influence mental health. In some cultures, mental health is stigmatized, making it difficult to seek help.

Stigma and Misconceptions Related to Mental Health

Despite growing awareness of mental health issues, stigma remains a significant obstacle for many people. Stigma can prevent people from reaching out for support and can perpetuate discrimination against those living with mental illness.

1. What Is Stigma?

Stigma refers to the negative views, beliefs, and stereotypes that society attaches to certain groups or conditions. In the context of mental health, stigma often manifests as judgment, misunderstanding, or fear directed at people with mental illness. There are two main types of stigma:

- **Public stigma:** The negative or discriminatory attitude that society holds toward people with mental illness. This can include stereotypes portraying them as dangerous, weak, or unable to contribute to society.

- **Self-stigma:** When people with mental health conditions internalize these negative beliefs, it can lead to feelings of shame, guilt, or embarrassment. Self-stigma can prevent people from seeking help or believing they deserve treatment.

2. Common Misconceptions About Mental Health

There are many misconceptions about mental health that lead to stigma. Here are some examples:

- **"Mental illness is a sign of weakness."** One of the most harmful misconceptions is that mental illness reflects personal failure or weakness. In reality, mental health issues are medical issues, and it takes strength and courage to seek help.

- **"People with mental illness are dangerous."** This stereotype is often perpetuated by media portrayals of people with mental illness as violent and unpredictable. In fact, most people with mental illness are not dangerous and are more likely to be victims of violence than perpetrators.

- **"Your mental health problems are all in your head."** Some people believe mental health problems aren't real, or that a person can simply "get over it." In fact, mental illnesses are rooted in complex biological, psychological, and social factors and require appropriate treatment and support.

- **"You don't need therapy or medication."** Another misconception is that mental illness can be solved through willpower alone. While self-help techniques are valuable, many people with mental health conditions benefit from therapy, medication, and professional treatment.

Conclusion

Understanding mental health is essential to developing a more compassionate and informed approach to well-being. Mental health is not just the absence of illness but a dynamic state of emotional, psychological, and social well-being that fluctuates over time. Recognizing the difference between mental health and mental illness helps us acknowledge that everyone has mental health needs, regardless of whether they have a formal diagnosis.

By examining common mental health issues such as depression, anxiety, and PTSD, we can better understand the challenges people face and the importance of early intervention and treatment.

Understanding the biological, psychological, and social factors that influence mental health also helps us appreciate the complexity of mental well-being and the need for a holistic approach to care.

Finally, tackling the stigma and misconceptions surrounding mental health is essential to encouraging more people to seek help and support. Challenging harmful stereotypes and encouraging open, honest conversations about mental health can help create a society where mental health is prioritized and everyone has the opportunity to thrive.

Chapter 2

The Invisible Struggle — Recognizing the Signs

Mental health problems often go unnoticed by others, and even those experiencing them may keep their struggles hidden beneath the surface. These problems can develop slowly in everyday life, appearing in subtle ways that are easy to overlook or misinterpret. By the time mental health concerns become severe enough to interfere with daily functioning, they can feel overwhelming and unmanageable. Recognizing the early signs of mental health challenges is crucial for preventing more serious issues down the road and for empowering individuals to seek help before their condition worsens. This chapter focuses on identifying the early warning signs of mental health issues, helping readers understand how these signs appear in people, and emphasizing the importance of early intervention. By better understanding the emotional, physical, and behavioural indicators of mental health struggles, people can more effectively support themselves and others who need timely care.

Mental health problems don't always show up in obvious ways. They can manifest as changes in emotions, physical sensations, and behaviour. These signs vary from person to person — what is an obvious warning sign for one person may not be for another — so understanding these different dimensions is essential to recognizing when something is wrong.

1. *Emotional Signs*

Emotional changes are often the most prominent indicators of mental health issues, but they can be difficult to interpret. Everyone experiences mood swings, but persistent or extreme emotional shifts may signal an underlying problem. Here are some common emotional signs of mental health issues:

- **Persistent sadness or hopelessness:** It's normal to feel down sometimes, but when sadness becomes overwhelming and lasts for weeks or months, it may be a sign of depression or another mood disorder. Those who experience this often describe it as a heavy emotional burden, a sense of hopelessness, or a feeling of "emptiness" inside.

- **Irritability and anger:** Increased irritability, frustration, or frequent outbursts of anger can be symptoms of a mental health problem such as anxiety or depression. These emotions may arise from an inability to cope with stress or from feelings of helplessness.

- **Anxiety or worry:** Everyone experiences anxiety from time to time, but when worry becomes excessive, constant, and uncontrollable, it may point to an anxiety disorder. People with anxiety often feel fearful or on edge about everyday situations, even when there is no imminent threat.

- **Feelings of guilt or worthlessness:** Excessive feelings of guilt, shame, or worthlessness can be a warning sign of depression. People may view themselves as failures or as undeserving of happiness or success, even when these thoughts are not based in reality.

- **Emotional numbness:** Some people with mental health issues don't feel intense sadness, anger, or anxiety, but instead experience emotional numbness. They may feel disconnected from their emotions and no longer enjoy activities they once loved. This emotional disconnection is often associated with trauma-related symptoms, including depression and PTSD.

2. Physical Signs

While mental health is primarily emotional and psychological, it often manifests through physical symptoms as well. The mind and body are deeply interconnected, and disruptions to mental health can cause physiological changes. Although these physical signs are often overlooked or attributed to other causes, they can be important clues to a person's overall health.

- **Chronic fatigue or lack of energy:** Feeling tired after a long day or week is normal, but persistent fatigue that doesn't improve with rest may indicate a mental health issue, especially depression or chronic stress. People with mental health issues often lack the energy to complete everyday tasks and may feel physically overwhelmed.

- **Changes in sleep patterns:** Sleep disturbances are common in people with mental health problems. Insomnia, hypersomnia (sleeping too much), or irregular sleep patterns can be signs of anxiety, depression, or stress. Many people with anxiety struggle to calm down at night, while those with depression may sleep excessively or experience restless sleep.

- **Unexplained pain:** Mental health issues can sometimes manifest as physical pain, such as headaches, muscle tension, or stomach problems. Stress and anxiety often lead to muscle tension and stiffness, while depression can cause general aches and pains. In some cases, these aches are linked to the body's stress response, since mental health issues can trigger the release of stress hormones like cortisol.

- **Changes in appetite or weight:** A sudden change in appetite — eating more or less than usual — can be a sign of a mental health problem. People with depression may lose interest in food, while others may use food as a way to cope with emotional stress. These dietary changes may also be accompanied by significant weight loss or gain.

- **Digestive issues:** The link between mental health and gut health is well documented, with anxiety, depression, and stress often manifesting as digestive issues such as nausea, diarrhoea, and irritable bowel syndrome (IBS). The gut-brain axis — the communication pathway between the brain and digestive system — means that mental health issues can produce physical symptoms in the digestive tract.

3. Behavioural Signs

Changes in behaviour can also signal the emergence of mental health issues. These changes aren't always obviously connected to mental health, but they can provide valuable clues about a person's emotional state.

- **Social withdrawal:** One of the most telling signs of mental health struggles is a change in social behaviour. People experiencing anxiety, depression, or other mental health issues often isolate themselves from friends, family, and social activities. They may avoid gatherings or lose interest in relationships.

- **Decreased productivity or performance:** Mental health problems can affect a person's ability to focus, concentrate, or complete tasks. This can lead to decreased productivity at work, school, or in personal responsibilities. Individuals may struggle to stay organized, meet deadlines, and manage tasks that previously seemed easy.

- **Procrastination and avoidance:** Procrastination and avoidance can become more pronounced when someone is struggling with their mental health. This behaviour can be triggered by fear of failure, feelings of inadequacy, or an inability to cope with stress. Tasks that were once routine can start to feel overwhelming and get avoided altogether.

- **Risky behaviour:** In some cases, people engage in risky behaviour to cope with or escape from their mental health issues. This can include reckless driving, gambling, substance use, or unsafe sexual behaviour. These actions can be a way of self-soothing or expressing emotional pain.

- **Substance abuse:** Many people with mental health problems turn to drugs or alcohol to cope with their emotions. While substance use may provide temporary relief, it often worsens mental health problems over time. Alcohol and drug abuse can create a cycle of dependency that exacerbates symptoms of anxiety, depression, and other conditions.

- **Self-harm:** Self-harming behaviours such as cutting, burning, or hitting oneself are dangerous and can indicate deep psychological distress. People who self-harm may do so to cope with overwhelming emotions or to express feelings they cannot put into words. Although self-harm is not necessarily associated with suicidal thoughts, it is a strong indicator that a person needs help.

Recognizing Anxiety, Depression, Stress, and Burnout

Mental health issues can take many forms, but anxiety, depression, stress, and burnout are among the most common conditions. While each of these conditions has its own characteristics, they can often overlap, making them difficult to differentiate. Recognizing the specific features of each can help people identify what they are experiencing and take steps to address it.

1. Recognizing Anxiety

Anxiety is a natural response to stress, but for some people it becomes overwhelming and persistent. Anxiety disorders, such as generalized anxiety disorder (GAD), panic disorder, and social anxiety disorder, are characterized by excessive worry or fear that interferes with daily life.

Common signs of anxiety include:

- **Constant worry:** People with anxiety often experience an overwhelming sense of worry, even about situations that may seem insignificant to others. This worry can be difficult to control and may focus on a variety of topics, from work or school to personal relationships and health.

- **Restlessness:** Anxiety can make it difficult to relax, leading to feelings of restlessness or being on edge. People with anxiety may find it hard to sit still or focus on tasks because their mind is constantly racing.

- **Physical symptoms:** Anxiety often comes with physical symptoms, such as a racing heart, sweating, trembling, or shortness of breath. These symptoms may occur during an anxiety attack or persist at a milder level throughout the day.

- **Avoidance behaviour:** People with anxiety disorders often go out of their way to avoid anxiety-provoking situations, such as social events, public speaking, or air travel. Although avoidance may provide short-term relief, it often increases anxiety in the long run.

- **Sleep problems:** Many people with anxiety have difficulty falling or staying asleep due to racing thoughts or physical discomfort. This can lead to fatigue and increased anxiety throughout the day.

2. Recognizing Depression

Depression is more than just feeling sad or going through a difficult time — it is a serious mood disorder that affects how a person feels, thinks, and functions. People with depression often experience deep feelings of hopelessness and worthlessness that make it difficult to function in daily life.

Common signs of depression include:

- **Persistent feelings of sadness or emptiness:** One of the hallmarks of depression is pervasive sadness, emptiness, or hopelessness that can last for weeks or months. People with depression may struggle to find joy in anything and may feel like they are constantly living under a cloud.

- **Loss of interest in activities:** People with depression often lose interest in activities they once enjoyed, such as hobbies, socializing, and exercise. This lack of interest, called anhedonia, can make it difficult to participate in everyday life.

- **Fatigue and lack of energy:** Depression can sap a person's energy, leaving them feeling physically and mentally exhausted. Simple tasks like getting out of bed or taking a shower can feel overwhelming.

- **Feelings of guilt or worthlessness:** People with depression often feel like failures or that they don't deserve to be happy. These feelings may be irrational, but they can be incredibly difficult to shake.

- **Thoughts of death or suicide:** In severe cases, depression can lead to thoughts of death or suicide. People experiencing these thoughts should seek professional help immediately, as depression is a serious condition that requires treatment.

3. Recognizing Stress

Stress is a normal part of life, but chronic or poorly managed stress can lead to significant mental and physical health problems. Stress occurs when a person feels overwhelmed by the demands placed on them, whether those demands relate to work, relationships, finances, or health.

Common signs of stress include:

- **Feeling overwhelmed:** People who are stressed may feel like they have too much to do and can't keep up with their responsibilities. This can lead to feelings of frustration, anxiety, and irritation.

- **Physical symptoms:** Stress often manifests as physical symptoms like headaches, muscle tension, stomach problems, and fatigue. If left unaddressed, these symptoms can worsen over time.

- **Decreased concentration:** Stress can make it difficult to focus on a task, leading to reduced productivity and efficiency. People under stress may be more easily distracted or forgetful.

- **Irritability and anger:** Chronic stress can make a person more irritable and easily angered, especially when they feel overwhelmed or unable to cope with their responsibilities.

- **Sleep problems:** Stress often disrupts sleep, making it hard to fall asleep or stay asleep. This can cause fatigue and worsen feelings of stress during the day.

4. Recognizing Burnout

Burnout is a state of emotional, physical, and mental exhaustion usually caused by prolonged stress related to work or caregiving responsibilities. It often develops when people feel overloaded by their obligations and unable to meet the demands placed on them.

Common signs of burnout include:

- **Emotional exhaustion:** People experiencing burnout often feel emotionally drained and unable to cope with their responsibilities. They may feel detached or apathetic toward their work or personal life.

- **Decline in performance:** Burnout can cause a significant drop in performance, as it becomes difficult to concentrate on tasks and meet deadlines.

- **Cynicism or detachment:** People experiencing burnout may become cynical about or detached from their work. They may feel like nothing they do matters and lose their sense of purpose and satisfaction.

- **Physical symptoms:** Burnout is often accompanied by physical symptoms such as headaches, muscle tension, fatigue, and insomnia. If left untreated, these symptoms can worsen over time.

- **Loss of motivation:** People experiencing burnout may lose the motivation to continue with work or personal responsibilities. They may feel like they are simply going through the motions, without any sense of fulfilment or satisfaction.

The Importance of Self-Awareness and Early Intervention

Recognizing the signs of mental health issues is only the first step toward addressing them. Self-awareness and early intervention are critical for managing mental health and preventing more serious problems from developing.

1. Cultivating Self-Awareness

Self-awareness is the ability to recognize and understand your own feelings, thoughts, and behaviours. This includes paying attention to how you feel physically and emotionally and how your actions affect your well-being. Building self-awareness is essential to recognizing the early signs of mental health issues and taking proactive steps to address them.

Strategies for building self-awareness include:

- **Mindfulness:** Practicing mindfulness involves focusing on the present moment without judgment. It can help you become more aware of your thoughts, emotions, and physical sensations, making it easier to recognize when something is off.

- **Journaling:** Writing down your thoughts and feelings can help you gain insight into your emotional state and identify patterns in your behaviour. Journaling is also a useful tool for managing difficult emotions and reducing stress.

- **Self-reflection:** Taking time to reflect on your experiences and their impact on your well-being can help you gain a deeper understanding of your mental health. This may include asking yourself questions like "How am I feeling today?" or "What's been stressing me out lately?"

2. Seek Help Early

One of the most important aspects of mental health is seeking help early. The sooner you address a mental health issue, the easier it will be to manage. Early intervention can prevent minor issues from becoming more serious problems and can improve overall outcomes.

If you recognize signs of mental health issues in yourself or others, it's important to take action. This may include talking to a trusted friend or family member, seeking help from a mental health professional, or making lifestyle changes to improve your well-being.

Here are some steps to seek help early:

- **Talk to someone:** If you are struggling with your mental health, reaching out to a trusted friend, family member, or colleague can provide valuable support. Talking about your feelings can help you gain perspective and feel less isolated.

- **Seek professional help:** If you are experiencing persistent or severe mental health symptoms, it is important to seek help from a mental health professional. A therapist, counsellor, or psychiatrist can give you the tools and support you need to manage your mental health.

- **Take care of yourself:** Maintaining your physical and emotional health is essential to supporting your mental health. This may mean getting sufficient sleep, eating balanced meals, exercising regularly, and making time for joy and relaxation.

Conclusion

The invisible struggles of mental health issues can be difficult to recognize, both in ourselves and in others. However, by becoming more aware of the emotional, physical, and behavioural signs of mental health issues, we can be more proactive about addressing these challenges before they become overwhelming.

Recognizing the signs of anxiety, depression, stress, and burnout is essential for early intervention and effective treatment. By building self-awareness and seeking help as early as possible, people can take control of their mental health and prevent minor issues from developing into more serious problems.

After all, mental health is an essential component of overall well-being, and it deserves the same attention as physical health. By recognizing the signs of mental health problems and taking steps to address them, we can lead healthier, happier lives and help the people around us do the same.

Chapter 3

The Power of Therapy — Professional Help and Its Impact

Mental health is a complex and multifaceted aspect of well-being that requires attention and care, just like physical health. Recognition of the importance of mental health has grown in recent years, and with it, awareness of the resources available to those who need support. Therapy has become one of the most powerful tools people can use to manage and improve their mental health.

Despite this growing awareness, stigma and misconceptions about therapy continue to create barriers that prevent people from seeking professional help. In this chapter, we will examine the power of therapy and professional mental health care, introduce the different types of therapy, explain how therapy works, consider the role of medication in mental health treatment, and discuss the value of support groups and peer support.

Benefits of Therapy and Professional Mental Health Care

Therapy provides a safe, structured environment in which people can explore their thoughts, feelings, and behaviours without judgment. Professional mental health care uses evidence-based approaches designed to help people overcome challenges, develop coping strategies, and ultimately live more fulfilling lives. Some of the main benefits of therapy and professional mental health care include:

1. Emotional Support

At its core, therapy provides emotional support. Many people seek therapy because they need a space to talk openly about their thoughts and feelings without fear of judgment. Therapists listen compassionately, validate the client's experience, and help them process difficult emotions.

2. Self-Awareness and Personal Growth

Therapy encourages introspection and self-awareness. By examining past experiences, thoughts, and patterns of behaviour, people can gain a deeper understanding of the root causes of their difficulties. This understanding allows them to make positive changes in their lives and grow emotionally and psychologically.

3. Developing Coping Skills

One of the most important benefits of therapy is developing coping skills. Whether you're dealing with anxiety, depression, trauma, stress, or anything else, therapy teaches practical tools and strategies for managing difficult emotions and situations. Over time, these skills can increase emotional stability and improve overall well-being.

4. Improved Relationships

Therapy not only helps people understand themselves better, it also improves how they interact with others. By working on communication skills, emotional regulation, and conflict resolution, therapy can lead to healthier, more fulfilling relationships with partners, family, friends, and colleagues.

5. Addressing Root Causes

There are often deep, underlying causes behind mental health struggles that are not immediately obvious. Therapy helps individuals uncover and address these root causes, whether they are linked to past trauma, unresolved grief, self-esteem issues, or deeply ingrained patterns of thinking. By addressing these underlying issues, therapy can support genuine healing and long-term transformation.

6. Breaking the Cycle of Negative Thinking

Negative thought patterns are common in many mental health conditions, especially anxiety and depression. These patterns can create a vicious cycle in which negative thoughts fuel negative feelings and behaviours. Therapy — particularly cognitive behavioural therapy (CBT) — is designed to help people break this cycle by challenging and reframing negative thoughts.

7. Prevention and Early Intervention

Therapy is not just for people in crisis; it is also a powerful tool for prevention and early intervention. Getting treatment early can help address mental health issues before they develop into more serious problems. Therapy can also provide ongoing support for those looking to maintain their mental health and well-being.

8. Increased Self-Confidence and Empowerment

As treatment progresses and people begin to understand themselves better, they often feel more confident and empowered. Therapy helps people recognize their strengths, increase their self-esteem, and believe in their ability to overcome challenges.

Different Types of Therapy

There are many different forms of therapy, each with its own approach and techniques. The type of therapy that is most effective depends on each individual's specific needs and preferences. Below we look at some of the most common forms of therapy, including cognitive behavioural therapy (CBT), dialectical behaviour therapy (DBT), psychodynamic therapy, humanistic therapy, and others.

1. Cognitive Behavioural Therapy (CBT)

Cognitive behavioural therapy (CBT) is one of the most widely used and studied forms of therapy. It is based on the idea that our thoughts, emotions, and behaviours are interconnected, and that negative thought patterns can lead to emotional distress and unhealthy behaviour.

Key elements of CBT:

- **Cognitive restructuring:** CBT focuses on identifying and addressing negative or distorted thoughts, also known as cognitive distortions. For example, someone with anxiety might think, "Something terrible is going to happen," or "I can't handle it." In CBT, the therapist helps the client reframe these thoughts in a more balanced and realistic way.

- **Behavioural interventions:** In addition to addressing negative thoughts, CBT also focuses on behavioural change. This may include developing coping strategies, gradually overcoming fears through exposure therapy, or practicing relaxation techniques to reduce anxiety.

- **Problem solving:** CBT teaches people how to approach problems in a more structured and effective way. This involves breaking down difficult problems into small, manageable steps and finding practical solutions. CBT is highly effective for a wide range of mental health conditions, including anxiety disorders, depression, PTSD, and obsessive-compulsive disorder (OCD).

2. Dialectical Behaviour Therapy (DBT)

Dialectical behaviour therapy (DBT) was originally developed to treat individuals with borderline personality disorder (BPD), but it has since been adapted to help people with a variety of mental health issues, including emotional dysregulation, self-harm, and eating disorders.

Key components of DBT:

- **Mindfulness:** DBT emphasizes mindfulness, which involves staying present in the moment and observing thoughts and emotions without judgment. It helps people become more aware of their emotional reactions and reduces impulsive responses.

- **Emotional regulation:** DBT teaches people how to recognize and manage intense emotions in healthy ways. This includes learning skills to reduce emotional vulnerability and build emotional resilience.

- **Interpersonal effectiveness:** DBT focuses on improving communication and relationship skills, helping individuals build healthier, more fulfilling connections. This includes learning how to set boundaries, assert needs, and resolve conflicts constructively.

- **Distress tolerance:** One unique aspect of DBT is its emphasis on distress tolerance skills, which teach individuals how to cope with difficult emotions and situations without resorting to harmful behaviours like self-harm or substance abuse.

3. Psychodynamic Therapy

Psychodynamic therapy is rooted in the theories of Sigmund Freud and focuses on exploring unconscious thoughts and emotions that influence behaviour. This type of therapy helps individuals gain insight into how past experiences, particularly childhood experiences, shape their current thoughts, emotions, and behaviours.

Key elements of psychodynamic therapy:

- **Exploring the unconscious:** Psychodynamic therapy helps people uncover unconscious thoughts, desires, and conflicts that may be influencing their behaviour. This process often involves discussing past experiences and relationships.

- **Transference and countertransference:** In psychodynamic therapy, the relationship between the therapist and the client is an important part of the healing process. Transference occurs when a client projects feelings from a past relationship onto the therapist, while countertransference occurs when the therapist reacts emotionally toward the client. Both are examined as part of the therapeutic process.

- **Insight and introspection:** The goal of psychodynamic therapy is to help people better understand their unconscious patterns and motivations. This self-awareness can lead to lasting changes in behaviour and emotional well-being.

4. Humanistic Therapy

Humanistic therapy is based on the belief that people have an innate capacity for self-development and self-actualization. This approach aims to help people build self-esteem and realize their full potential. Humanistic therapy is client-centered and emphasizes empathy, acceptance, and unconditional positive regard on the part of the therapist.

Key elements of humanistic therapy:

- **Client-centered therapy:** Humanistic therapy, particularly Carl Rogers' client-centered therapy, emphasizes the importance of creating a supportive, non-judgmental therapeutic environment. Therapists provide unconditional positive regard, empathy, and genuine understanding so that clients feel heard and valued.

- **Self-actualization:** Humanistic therapy encourages individuals to explore their own values, goals, and aspirations. The goal is to help clients achieve self-actualization — the process of becoming their best self.

- **Focus on the present:** Unlike psychodynamic therapy, which often focuses on the past, humanistic therapy emphasizes the present moment and the client's current experience. Therapists encourage clients to take responsibility for their choices and focus on personal growth.

5. Other Forms of Therapy

In addition to CBT, DBT, psychodynamic therapy, and humanistic therapy, there are many other forms of treatment that can be useful for people with different needs.

- **Acceptance and Commitment Therapy (ACT):** ACT is a form of therapy that focuses on accepting difficult emotions and thoughts rather than avoiding or trying to control them. It encourages people to take meaningful action in line with their values, despite emotional discomfort.

- **Eye Movement Desensitization and Reprocessing (EMDR):** EMDR is a specialized treatment used primarily for trauma and PTSD. It involves using bilateral stimulation, such as guided eye movements or tapping, while a person processes traumatic memories. This helps reduce the emotional intensity of the memory and promotes healing.

- **Family therapy:** Family therapy involves working with families to improve communication, resolve conflicts, and strengthen relationships. This type of therapy is often used to address issues such as parenting challenges, family dynamics, and the impact of mental health problems on the family unit.

- **Group therapy:** Group therapy involves working with a therapist alongside other people facing similar issues. This provides peer support, an opportunity to share experiences, and a chance to learn from others.

How Therapy Works: Overcoming Stigma

Despite increasing awareness of the importance of treatment, stigma surrounding mental health care remains. Many people view asking for help as a sign of weakness and may avoid getting the support they need. Addressing this stigma is essential to building a culture of openness, acceptance, and understanding around mental health issues.

The Therapeutic Relationship

The therapeutic relationship is one of the most important factors influencing the effectiveness of therapy. A strong alliance between client and therapist fosters trust, empathy, and understanding, creating a safe space for individuals to explore their thoughts and emotions.

Elements of a positive therapeutic relationship:

- **Trust:** Clients must trust that their therapist is genuinely interested in their well-being and that the therapeutic space is confidential.

- **Empathy:** A therapist's ability to understand and resonate with a client's emotions fosters deeper connection and allows for more meaningful exploration of emotional issues.

- **A non-judgmental attitude:** A supportive, accepting environment encourages clients to share their experiences without fear of criticism or shame.

The Therapeutic Process

The therapeutic process is usually divided into several stages, each contributing to the client's growth and development.

- **1. Initial assessment:** During the first session, the therapist gathers information about the client's background, presenting problems, and treatment goals. This assessment lays the foundation for treatment.

- **2. Exploration:** Clients share their thoughts and feelings, exploring their experiences and patterns of behaviour. This phase helps identify key issues and concerns that need to be addressed.

- **3. Insight and understanding:** As treatment progresses, clients gain insight into their own mental processes, identify the underlying factors contributing to their struggles, and better understand the reasons behind their actions.

- **4. Action and change:** In the final phase, clients work with their therapist to develop and implement strategies for change. This can include practicing new skills, setting goals, and monitoring progress.

Benefits of Therapy

Participating in therapy can offer many benefits beyond symptom relief. Some of the most important include:

- **Improved coping skills:** Therapy gives people the tools to manage stress and deal effectively with life's challenges.

- **Enhanced self-awareness:** Clients gain insight into their thoughts, emotions, and behaviours, fostering personal growth and self-discovery.

- **Emotional resilience:** Therapy promotes emotional regulation, helping individuals build resilience in the face of adversity.

- **Improved relationships:** Therapy can improve relationships with family, friends, and partners by strengthening communication and interpersonal skills.

- **Increased overall well-being:** Many people report a better quality of life and greater satisfaction after receiving treatment.

By understanding how therapy works and the benefits it provides, individuals can move past stigma and embrace the journey toward better mental health.

The Role of Medication in Mental Health Treatment

Therapy is a powerful tool for addressing mental health problems, but medication often plays an important role in treatment as well. Understanding the role of medication is essential to taking a comprehensive approach to mental health care.

Psychopharmacology

Psychopharmacology involves the study and use of medication to treat mental health disorders. Different classes of psychiatric medications target different symptoms and conditions, providing symptom relief for many people.

Common classes of psychiatric medications:

- **1. Antidepressants:** These medications are generally used to treat depression and anxiety disorders. They work by altering the levels of certain neurotransmitters in the brain, helping to reduce symptoms.

- **2. Antipsychotics:** Primarily prescribed for schizophrenia and bipolar disorder, antipsychotics help manage symptoms such as hallucinations and delusions.

- **3. Mood stabilizers:** Often used for people with bipolar disorder, mood stabilizers help regulate mood swings and prevent manic or depressive episodes.

- **4. Anti-anxiety medications:** These medications can provide short-term relief from severe anxiety symptoms.

Combined Treatment: Medication and Therapy

For many people, combining therapy and medication offers the most effective approach to treatment. While therapy addresses the emotional and psychological aspects of mental health, medication can provide the biochemical support needed to manage symptoms.

Benefits of combined treatment:

- **1. Symptom reduction:** Medication can reduce symptoms enough to allow people to participate more fully in — and benefit more from — therapy.

- **2. Increased effectiveness:** Research has shown that combining therapy and medication, especially for severe depression or anxiety, can produce the best outcomes for many mental health conditions.

- **3. Integrated care:** A holistic approach that addresses both psychological and physiological factors promotes overall well-being.

Considerations and Controversies

Despite the benefits of medication, the topic of psychiatric medication often raises concerns. The use of medication to treat mental health issues remains stigmatized by some, who view it as a crutch rather than a legitimate form of care. Additionally, the potential for side effects and the importance of informed consent are critical factors in the decision-making process.

Key considerations:

- **1. Informed consent:** Clients should clearly understand the benefits, risks, and potential side effects of medication before starting treatment. This allows individuals to make informed decisions about their care.

- **2. Monitoring and adjustments:** Regular follow-up visits with a healthcare provider are important for monitoring progress and making any necessary adjustments to the treatment plan, ensuring clients receive care tailored to their changing needs.

Support Groups and Peer Support

In addition to therapy and medication, support groups and peer support play an important role in mental health care. These community-based resources give people a sense of belonging and understanding as they navigate mental health issues.

Definition and Purpose

Support groups bring together people facing similar challenges to share experiences, offer support, and learn from one another. These groups are led by mental health professionals or peer facilitators who have lived experience with mental health issues.

Benefits of Support Groups

- **1. Shared experience:** Connecting with others who understand their difficulties can reduce feelings of isolation and loneliness. Participants often find comfort in knowing they are not alone in their experiences.

- **2. Empowerment:** Sharing stories and strategies promotes empowerment and encourages people to take an active role in their recovery. Participants can discover new ways of coping and gain hope from the experiences of others.

- **3. Access to resources:** Support groups often provide additional resources, coping strategies, and information about mental health services to help people make informed decisions about treatment.

- **4. Skills development:** Many support groups include an educational component that teaches participants about mental health, self-care, and effective coping strategies.

Effectiveness and Accessibility

Research shows that support groups can be an effective complement to individual therapy. They provide a platform for people to practice new skills, receive feedback, and build social connections — all of which are essential to mental health recovery.

The rise of technology has led to a proliferation of online support groups, making mental health resources more accessible than ever before. These platforms allow individuals to connect with others regardless of geographic location and help break down barriers to support.

Peer support programs involve individuals who have been trained to provide support to others facing similar issues. These peer supporters often share personal experiences, coping strategies, and resources to promote hope and resilience.

Conclusion

The power of therapy lies in its ability to promote healing, growth, and resilience. As awareness of mental health complexity grows, so does recognition of the value of professional support. Through therapy in its various forms, people can gain understanding, build coping skills, and develop meaningful connections. While therapy is a powerful tool on its own, it is often complemented by medication and peer support to create a holistic approach to mental health care. As we continue to break down the stigma surrounding mental health and help-seeking behaviour, it is crucial to recognize therapy as a valuable resource. By prioritizing mental health care and advocating for support, we can empower individuals to take charge of their mental well-being and lead fulfilling lives.

In a world where mental health challenges are common, understanding the power of therapy is more important than ever. With the right support, individuals can embark on a transformative journey toward healing and self-discovery — ultimately enriching their own lives and the lives of those around them.

Chapter 4

Mindfulness and Meditation — Tools for Everyday Mental Health

Introduction to Mindfulness and Meditation

Mindfulness and meditation have gained popularity in recent years, not only as spiritual practices but also as evidence-based tools for improving mental health and overall well-being. These practices are known for their ability to reduce stress, improve emotional regulation, increase self-awareness, and promote a sense of inner peace. Mindfulness refers to the practice of being fully present and engaged in the current moment without judgment, while meditation is a more formal practice that often involves focusing the mind on a particular object, thought, or activity to achieve mental clarity and emotional calm. Combining mindfulness and meditation provides a powerful tool for managing mental health, reducing anxiety and overthinking, and increasing emotional resilience.

In this chapter, we look at the science of mindfulness and its effects on the brain, guided mindfulness practices and meditation techniques, how mindfulness can reduce stress and anxiety, and practical ways to incorporate mindfulness into your daily life.

The Science of Mindfulness: Its Effects on the Brain

Over the past few decades, research into the effects of mindfulness and meditation on the brain has increased significantly. The evidence is clear: practicing mindfulness leads to measurable changes in brain structure and function that promote improved mental health and emotional well-being.

1. Mindfulness and Neuroplasticity

Neuroplasticity refers to the brain's ability to change and adapt in response to experience. Mindfulness and meditation have been shown to improve neuroplasticity, especially in areas of the brain involved in attention, emotion regulation, and self-awareness.

One of the primary areas affected by mindfulness is the prefrontal cortex, which is responsible for higher-order thinking, decision-making, and emotional control. Regular mindfulness practice strengthens this part of the brain, promoting better focus, emotional regulation, and more conscious decision-making.

2. The Amygdala and Stress Regulation

The amygdala is a part of the brain involved in processing emotions, particularly fear and stress. It plays a central role in the body's physical stress response, triggering the "fight or flight" reaction when it perceives a threat. However, in people with chronic stress, anxiety, or trauma, the amygdala can become overactive, leading to heightened anxiety and stress levels.

Research has shown that mindfulness and meditation can reduce the size and activity of the amygdala, helping to calm the stress response. This can lower overall anxiety levels and help people respond more calmly and clearly to stressful situations.

3. The Default Mode Network and Rumination

The default mode network (DMN) is a network of brain regions that becomes active when the mind is at rest or wandering — often when we are lost in thought, worry, or rumination. This network is closely associated with patterns of self-focused and negative thinking. Research has shown that mindfulness and meditation quiet the DMN, reducing rumination on negative thoughts and the tendency to dwell on them. By training attention on the present moment, mindfulness can help interrupt cycles of repetitive thinking, allowing people to feel greater mental clarity and emotional balance.

4. Improved Emotion Regulation

Mindfulness can help improve emotion regulation by increasing activity in the anterior cingulate cortex and insula, brain regions involved in processing emotions and bodily sensations. This increased awareness of emotions and physical sensations allows people to recognize and respond more effectively to emotional triggers, reducing the risk of impulsive or reactive behaviour.

In short, mindfulness and meditation produce important changes in the brain that improve emotional regulation, reduce stress and anxiety, and enhance overall mental health.

These changes occur because of the brain's remarkable ability to adapt and reorganize itself in response to new experiences.

Guided Mindfulness Practices and Meditation Techniques

While mindfulness and meditation may seem abstract or difficult for beginners, they are actually simple practices that, with a little guidance, can be incorporated into everyday life. Below are some common mindfulness practices and meditation techniques that can help people develop and benefit from mindfulness.

1. Basic Mindfulness Meditation

Mindfulness meditation is one of the easiest and most effective ways to practice mindfulness. It involves focusing on your breath, bodily sensations, or a specific object, and gently bringing your mind back to the present moment whenever it wanders.

How to practice basic mindfulness meditation:

- Find a quiet, comfortable place to sit or lie down.

- Close your eyes, take a few deep breaths, and relax.

- Focus on your breathing, noticing the sensations of air moving in and out of your nostrils and the rise and fall of your chest.

- When your mind wanders — and it will — gently bring your attention back to your breath without judgment.

- Continue this practice for 5–10 minutes, gradually increasing the time as you become more comfortable with it.

This simple practice helps train your mind to stay focused on the present moment, reducing the tendency to ruminate or become overwhelmed by anxious thoughts.

2. Body Scan Meditation

A body scan is a mindfulness practice that brings awareness to different parts of the body, noticing and releasing tension along the way. This practice is especially useful for reducing physical tension and stress.

How to practice body scan meditation:

- Lie down in a comfortable position and close your eyes.

- Take a few deep breaths and relax your body.

- Start by focusing on your feet. Notice any sensations — warmth, tension, discomfort — and simply observe without judgment.

- Slowly move your attention up your body, from your feet to your calves, thighs, abdomen, chest, arms, and head, spending a few moments on each area.

- As you focus on each part of your body, consciously release any tension you feel.

Body scan meditation cultivates a sense of mind-body connection and promotes relaxation and stress relief.

3. Loving-Kindness Meditation

Loving-kindness meditation, also known as metta meditation, is a practice focused on cultivating compassion and kindness toward oneself and others. It involves silently repeating phrases of goodwill, such as "May you be happy, may you be healthy, may you have peace," while extending these wishes to loved ones, acquaintances, and even people with whom you may be in conflict.

How to practice loving-kindness meditation:

- Sit comfortably and close your eyes.

- Begin by focusing on yourself. Silently repeat phrases of goodwill, such as "May I be happy, may I be safe, may I be at peace."

- After a moment, focus on a loved one and repeat the same phrases: "May you be happy, may you be healthy, may you be at peace."

- Gradually widen your circle of compassion by extending your wishes to acquaintances, strangers, and even people with whom you may be in conflict.

- Complete the meditation by extending the same wishes to all beings: "May all beings be happy, may all beings be safe, may all beings be at peace."

Loving-kindness meditation helps build the empathy, compassion, and emotional stability needed for better mental health and stronger relationships.

4. Walking Meditation

Walking meditation combines mindfulness and movement, making it a great option for people who find sitting meditation difficult. In this practice, you walk slowly and mindfully, paying close attention to each step and the sensations in your body.

How to practice walking meditation:

- Find a quiet place where you can walk without distraction.

- Begin by standing still, taking a few deep breaths, and centering yourself.

- As you begin to walk, focus on the sensation of your feet touching the ground.

- Walk slowly and deliberately, paying attention to each step, the movement of your feet, and the shifting of your weight.

- If your mind begins to wander, gently bring your attention back to the act of walking.

Walking meditation helps you incorporate mindfulness into your daily activities, promoting a sense of calm and groundedness.

5. *Mindful Breathing*

Mindful breathing is one of the simplest and most accessible mindfulness practices. It involves focusing on your breath and using it as an anchor to stay present in the moment.

How to practice mindful breathing:

- Sit or lie in a comfortable position.

- Close your eyes, take a few deep breaths, and relax.

- Focus your attention on your breath, noticing the sensations of air moving in and out of your body.

- When your mind wanders, gently bring it back to the feeling of your breath.

Mindful breathing can be practiced anywhere and at any time, making it an excellent tool for managing stress and anxiety throughout the day.

How Mindfulness Reduces Stress, Anxiety, and Overthinking

Mindfulness has been shown to reduce stress, anxiety, and overthinking through several key mechanisms. By focusing on the present moment, mindfulness helps individuals break free from the cycle of negative thinking and emotional distress that often accompanies stress and anxiety.

1. Mindfulness Reduces the Stress Response

As described above, regular mindfulness practice reduces activity in the amygdala, the part of the brain involved in the fight-or-flight response. This decrease in amygdala activity is associated with lower cortisol levels and a calmer overall stress response. Through mindfulness, people learn to notice their stress reactions with greater awareness and self-control, rather than responding impulsively or emotionally. This leads to a more measured response to stressful situations and reduces the overall toll stress takes on mental and physical health.

2. Mindfulness Breaks the Cycle of Overthinking

Overthinking, also known as rumination, is a common symptom of anxiety and depression. It involves repeatedly focusing on negative thoughts or problems, which can lead to increased stress and emotional exhaustion. Mindfulness helps break this cycle by bringing attention back to the present moment. Practicing mindfulness helps you notice when your mind is wandering or dwelling on negative thoughts, and gently redirect your attention back to the present. Over time, this habit can reduce the frequency and intensity of overthinking, leading to greater mental clarity and emotional balance.

3. Mindfulness Improves Emotional Regulation

One of the main benefits of mindfulness is its ability to improve emotional regulation. By increasing awareness of our emotions and physical sensations, mindfulness helps us recognize emotional triggers before they escalate into overwhelming reactions. This awareness gives us the opportunity to respond more thoughtfully and constructively to our emotions, rather than being ruled by them. For example, mindfulness can help someone recognize the early signs of anxiety or frustration, allowing them to take a few deep breaths or engage in a calming activity before their emotions become unmanageable.

4. Mindfulness Reduces Anxiety

Anxiety is often rooted in worry about the future and fear of the unknown. Mindfulness reduces anxiety by encouraging people to focus on the present moment rather than dwelling on what might happen. By staying grounded in the here and now, mindfulness helps quiet the mental chatter that fuels anxiety. It also helps individuals develop a sense of acceptance and non-judgment toward their thoughts and emotions, which can reduce the intensity of anxious feelings.

Incorporating Mindfulness into Your Daily Life

While a formal meditation practice offers significant benefits, weaving mindfulness into your daily life can further improve your mental health and overall well-being. This section provides practical strategies for incorporating mindfulness throughout your day.

A Mindful Morning Routine

Starting the day with mindfulness can set a positive tone for what follows. Here are some practices to consider:

- **1. Mindful waking:** When you wake up, take a moment to notice you're breathing and set your intentions for the day. Think about how you want to feel and what you want to focus on.

- **2. Mindful eating:** Practice mindful eating during breakfast by savouring every bite. Notice the taste, texture, and aroma of the food, and take your time to enjoy the experience.

- **3. Mindful movement:** Incorporate mindfulness into your morning exercise routine, whether that's yoga, stretching, or walking. Focus on the sensations of movement and your connection to your body and breath.

A Mindful Work Environment

Incorporating mindfulness into the workplace can improve focus and productivity while reducing stress.

- **1. Mindful breaks:** Take short, mindful breaks throughout the day. Step away from your desk, close your eyes, and take a few deep breaths. Use this time to recharge and reset your focus.

- **2. Mindful communication:** Practice active listening while talking with colleagues. Be fully present and focus on what the other person is saying without preparing your response in advance.

- **3. Gratitude practice:** At the end of your day, take a moment to think of three things you are grateful for. This practice can shift your thinking and promote a sense of gratitude.

A Mindful Evening Routine

Cultivating mindfulness in the evening can promote relaxation and prepare you for a restful night's sleep.

- **1. Digital detox:** Set aside time in the evening to disconnect from digital devices. Use this time for mindful activities like reading, journaling, or meditating.

- **2. Mindful reflection:** Before you go to bed, reflect on your day with gratitude and acceptance. Think about the challenges you faced and what you learned from them.

- **3. Relaxation techniques:** Incorporate relaxation techniques such as gentle stretching, deep breathing, or progressive muscle relaxation to unwind and prepare for sleep.

Mindfulness in Everyday Activities

Mindfulness can also be practiced during routine activities, turning mundane tasks into opportunities for presence and awareness.

- **1. Mindful showering:** Pay attention to the feeling of the water on your skin, the sound of the shower, and the smell of the soap and shampoo.

- **2. Mindful commuting:** Whether you're in a car, on a bike, or on public transport, practice mindful awareness by focusing on your breathing and your surroundings. Observe the sights, sounds, and smells without judgment.

- **3. Mindful housework:** Turn chores into mindful moments by focusing on the sensations and movements involved. Notice the texture of the dishes, the scent of the cleaner, or the rhythm of your movements.

Conclusion

Mindfulness and meditation are powerful tools for improving mental health and emotional regulation. The science behind these practices reveals their profound impact on the brain — contributing to emotional stability, reducing stress and anxiety, and fostering self-awareness. By incorporating mindfulness into daily life, people can feel more present, clear-headed, and content.

As we face the challenges of modern life, embracing mindfulness can open the door to emotional balance and mental health. With practice and dedication, people can harness the transformative power of mindfulness and meditation to lead more fulfilling and meaningful lives. In a world filled with distractions, the practice of presence can serve as a source of hope and healing, allowing people to navigate their mental health journey with grace and resilience.

Chapter 5

The Role of Lifestyle — Exercise, Sleep, and Nutrition

Introduction to the Mind-Body Connection

Mental health and physical health are often treated as separate concerns, but they are deeply linked, each influencing and supporting the other. A growing body of scientific evidence suggests that lifestyle factors such as exercise, sleep, and nutrition have a significant impact on mental well-being. These factors not only contribute to overall physical health but also play a key role in regulating mood, energy levels, and mental stability. Taking care of your body through exercise, adequate sleep, and a balanced diet leaves you better equipped to handle life's stressors and maintain a healthier, more positive outlook. In this chapter, we will examine the mind-body connection and look at the specific ways that exercise, sleep, and nutrition affect mental health.

Key topics will include how exercise improves mood and reduces stress through the release of endorphins, the importance of sleep hygiene for emotional regulation and cognitive function, and the important role of nutrition in brain health, particularly through the gut-brain axis. Understanding these relationships empowers individuals to make healthier lifestyle choices that positively impact both their physical and mental health.

The Mind-Body Connection: A Holistic View

The idea that the mind and body are interconnected is not new. Ancient philosophies and holistic health systems such as Ayurveda and Traditional Chinese Medicine have long emphasized this connection. Modern science now offers concrete evidence that our mental and emotional health is intimately linked to our physical health. This relationship is bidirectional, meaning our mental state can affect our physical health, and vice versa.

For example, chronic stress can lead to physical ailments such as high blood pressure, heart disease, and digestive problems, while physical conditions such as chronic pain or fatigue can contribute to feelings of anxiety, depression, and emotional distress. Conversely, taking care of our physical health through regular exercise, proper nutrition, and sufficient sleep can help protect against mental health challenges and promote a sense of well-being.

1. The Impact of Chronic Stress on Physical Health

Chronic stress is one of the most common threats to both mental and physical health. When we feel stressed, our bodies produce hormones like cortisol and adrenaline to prepare us to respond to a perceived threat. This fight-or-flight response is adaptive in the short term, but when stress becomes chronic, it can wreak havoc on the body and mind. Long-term exposure to stress hormones can lead to inflammation, weakened immune function, and an increased risk of developing diseases like heart disease, obesity, and diabetes. Chronic stress also has a significant impact on mental health, contributing to anxiety, depression, and burnout.

2. Physical Health as a Foundation for Mental Stability

Just as chronic stress can damage physical health, taking care of the body through a healthy lifestyle can build resilience for mental stability. Exercise, sleep, and nutrition are the pillars of physical health, and they provide the foundation for a balanced, well-functioning mind.

Regular physical activity has been shown to reduce symptoms of depression and anxiety, improve mood, and enhance cognitive function. Similarly, sufficient sleep is essential for emotional regulation, memory consolidation, and mental clarity.

Finally, a balanced diet that provides essential nutrients supports brain health, improves energy levels, and promotes emotional stability. Understanding the mind-body connection can help you see how your lifestyle choices impact both your mental and physical health. In the sections that follow, we'll look at the specific roles of exercise, sleep, and nutrition in mental health and offer practical tips for incorporating these habits into your daily life.

How Exercise Improves Mental Health

Exercise is often praised for its physical health benefits, such as improving cardiovascular fitness, building muscle, and supporting weight management. But the mental health benefits of exercise are just as significant — arguably more so. Regular physical activity has been shown to reduce symptoms of depression, anxiety, and stress, improve mood and self-esteem, and enhance cognitive function.

1. The Science Behind Exercise and Mental Health

When we engage in physical activity, our bodies release a cascade of chemicals that have a positive effect on the brain. One of the most well-known is endorphins, often called the body's natural "feel-good" hormones. Endorphins act as natural painkillers and mood enhancers, producing feelings of euphoria and reducing the perception of pain. In addition to endorphins, exercise also stimulates the production of other important brain chemicals, such as dopamine, serotonin, and norepinephrine, which play key roles in mood regulation and mental health. People with depression and anxiety often have an imbalance in these neurotransmitters, and regular exercise can help restore them to a more optimal state.

2. Reducing Stress Through Physical Activity

Physical exercise is one of the most effective ways to combat stress. Physical activity helps lower levels of the stress hormone cortisol while promoting the release of endorphins and other mood-boosting chemicals. Regular exercise can also improve the body's ability to respond to stress by strengthening the cardiovascular system, boosting immune function, and promoting relaxation. Exercise is also a healthy way to release pent-up energy and tension, making feelings of frustration, anger, and anxiety easier to manage. Whether it's jogging, yoga, or weightlifting, physical activity offers a constructive outlet for stress, leaving people feeling more balanced and less overwhelmed.

3. Exercise as a Natural Antidepressant

Numerous studies have shown that exercise can be as effective as medication in treating mild to moderate depression. Some researchers even call it a "natural antidepressant," due to its ability to raise levels of serotonin and dopamine in the brain. These neurotransmitters are often depleted in depression, and increasing their levels can improve mood and reduce feelings of sadness and despair. Exercise also promotes neurogenesis, the growth of new brain cells, particularly in the hippocampus — a region of the brain that is often smaller in people with depression. By stimulating the growth of new neurons in the hippocampus, exercise may help reverse some of the structural changes associated with depression.

4. Improved Cognitive Function and Mental Clarity

In addition to improving mood, exercise has been shown to enhance cognitive function, boost memory, and increase mental clarity. Physical activity increases blood flow to the brain, delivering more oxygen and nutrients to support optimal brain function.

Exercise also promotes the release of brain-derived neurotrophic factor (BDNF), a protein that supports the growth and survival of neurons and improves synaptic plasticity — the brain's ability to form new connections. This leads to improved learning, memory, and problem-solving skills, making exercise an important tool for maintaining cognitive health as we age.

5. Types of Exercise for Mental Health

While all forms of physical activity are beneficial for mental health, some types of exercise may be particularly effective for reducing stress, anxiety, and depression, including:

- **Aerobic exercise:** Activities such as running, swimming, cycling, and dancing are known to boost endorphin levels and improve mood. Aerobic exercise also supports cardiovascular health, which is closely linked to brain function.

- **Strength training:** Lifting weights or engaging in resistance exercises can improve self-esteem and body image while reducing symptoms of anxiety and depression.

- **Yoga:** Yoga combines physical movement with mindfulness and deep breathing, making it a powerful tool for reducing stress and promoting relaxation.

- **Mindful movement:** Activities like tai chi or Pilates focus on slow, controlled movements and breath awareness, helping to reduce anxiety and improve mental focus.

The key to reaping the mental health benefits of exercise is consistency. Even small amounts of physical activity, such as a 10-minute walk or a short stretching routine, can make a difference in mood and well-being.

Sleep Hygiene and Its Role in Emotional Regulation

Sleep is sometimes referred to as the "third pillar" of health, alongside diet and exercise. Sleep plays a key role in regulating mood, memory, and cognitive function, and poor sleep is associated with many mental health problems, including anxiety, depression, and mood disorders.

Maintaining good sleep hygiene — healthy habits that promote restful sleep — is essential to mental and emotional well-being.

1. The Relationship Between Sleep and Mental Health

The relationship between sleep and mental health is bidirectional: poor sleep can contribute to the development of mental health problems, and mental health problems can interfere with sleep. For example, people with anxiety disorders often have difficulty falling and staying asleep because of racing thoughts and restlessness. Similarly, depression is associated with both insomnia and hypersomnia (excessive sleep), further complicating the relationship between sleep and mood.

During sleep, the brain processes emotions, consolidates memories, and clears out toxins that build up during the day. Insufficient sleep disrupts emotional regulation, leading to increased irritability, difficulty concentrating, and elevated stress levels. Over time, chronic lack of sleep can worsen symptoms of anxiety and depression and increase the risk of developing more serious mental health disorders.

2. Sleep Stages and Their Importance

Sleep is divided into several stages, each of which plays a unique role in maintaining mental and physical health:

- **Stage 1 (light sleep):** The transition from wakefulness to sleep. During this stage, the body relaxes and begins to slow down.

- **Stage 2 (moderate sleep):** A deeper phase of sleep characterized by slower brain waves and a reduced heart rate. This stage is important for physical recovery and energy conservation.

- **Stage 3 (deep sleep):** Also known as slow-wave sleep, this stage is essential for physical recovery, immune function, and growth. Deep sleep is also critical for memory consolidation and emotional regulation.

- **REM sleep:** This is the stage of sleep during which most dreaming occurs. REM sleep is important for cognitive function, emotional processing, and problem-solving.

Each stage of sleep serves a specific purpose, and disruptions to your sleep cycle can negatively impact your mental and emotional health. For example, sleep deprivation is linked to increased emotional reactivity and greater difficulty regulating negative emotions.

3. Tips to Improve Sleep Hygiene

Improving sleep hygiene can help people get the restful, restorative sleep they need to maintain their mental health. Here are some tips:

- **Establish a consistent sleep schedule:** Going to bed and waking up at the same time every day, even on weekends, helps regulate your body's internal clock and improve sleep quality.

- **Create a relaxing bedtime routine:** Calming activities before bed, such as reading, meditating, or taking a warm bath, signal to your brain that it's time to wind down and prepare for sleep.

- **Limit screen exposure:** blue light emitted by phones, computers, and TVs can interfere with the production of melatonin, a hormone that regulates sleep. It's best to avoid screen time for at least an hour before bedtime.

- **Create a comfortable sleep environment:** A cool, dark, and quiet bedroom will help you sleep better. Blackout curtains, earplugs, and white noise machines can all help reduce disruptions.

- **Avoid caffeine and large meals before bed:** Caffeine and large meals can affect your ability to fall asleep and stay asleep. It's best to avoid both in the hours before bedtime.

By prioritizing sleep hygiene, people can improve their emotional regulation, cognitive function, and overall mental health.

Nutrition and Brain Health: The Gut-Brain Axis

The food we eat has a profound effect on our physical and mental health, and emerging research suggests that the relationship between diet and mental health may be mediated by the gut-brain axis. This gut-brain communication network plays a key role in regulating mood, stress response, and cognitive function.

1. The Gut-Brain Axis Explained

The gut-brain axis refers to the two-way communication between the digestive system (the gut) and the central nervous system (the brain). This communication occurs through several pathways, including the vagus nerve (the body's main parasympathetic nerve), immune system signalling, and the release of hormones and neurotransmitters. The gut is home to billions of microorganisms, collectively known as the gut microbiome, which play a key role in digestion, immune function, and the production of certain neurotransmitters, such as serotonin and dopamine. In fact, around 90% of the body's serotonin is produced in the gut, highlighting the important connection between gut health and mental health.

2. How Diet Impacts Mental Health

A healthy, balanced diet supports brain and mental health by providing the nutrients needed for neurotransmitter production, reducing inflammation, and protecting against oxidative stress. Conversely, a poor diet high in processed foods, sugar, and unhealthy fats can promote inflammation, oxidative stress, and imbalances in the gut microbiome — all of which can contribute to mental health issues.

Nutrients essential for brain health include:

- **Omega-3 fatty acids:** Found in fatty fish (such as salmon), flaxseeds, and walnuts, omega-3s are essential for brain function and have been shown to reduce symptoms of depression.

- **Antioxidants:** Foods rich in antioxidants, such as berries, dark leafy greens, and nuts, help protect the brain from oxidative stress and inflammation.

- **B vitamins:** Particularly folic acid, vitamin B12, and vitamin B6, these play an important role in neurotransmitter production and have been linked to improved mood and cognitive function.

- **Probiotics:** Foods containing beneficial bacteria, such as yogurt, kefir, and fermented vegetables, can support a healthy gut microbiome and promote the production of mood-regulating neurotransmitters.

3. *The Impact of Gut Health on Mental Well-Being*

The health of the gut microbiome has a significant impact on mental health, and an imbalance of gut flora (a condition known as dysbiosis) is associated with conditions such as depression, anxiety, and cognitive decline. A diet rich in fiber, prebiotics, and probiotics can help maintain a healthy gut microbiome and improve gut-brain communication. In addition to eating a balanced diet, you can support your gut health in the following ways:

- **Reduce stress:** Chronic stress can negatively impact gut health by altering the composition of the gut microbiome and promoting inflammation.

- **Drink enough water:** Proper hydration is essential for digestion and a healthy gut-brain axis.

- **Avoid overusing antibiotics:** While antibiotics may be necessary to treat infections, overuse can disrupt the balance of gut bacteria.

By nourishing both the gut and the brain, individuals can improve their mental resilience and emotional well-being.

Conclusion: Building a Healthy Lifestyle for Mental Well-Being

Exercise, sleep, and nutrition are powerful tools for promoting mental health and building emotional resilience. By prioritizing physical health and making intentional lifestyle choices, individuals can improve their mood, reduce stress and anxiety, and protect against mental health challenges. Understanding the mind-body connection and the role lifestyle factors play in mental well-being empowers individuals to take proactive steps toward a healthier, more balanced life.

Incorporating regular exercise, practicing good sleep hygiene, and nourishing the body with a balanced diet rich in brain-boosting nutrients are all essential components of a lifestyle that supports mental health. By making small, sustainable changes to daily habits, individuals can cultivate both physical and mental well-being and enjoy a greater sense of overall fulfilment and happiness.

Chapter 6

Building Resilience — Coping Strategies and Emotional Strength

Introduction to Resilience and Its Importance

Resilience is the ability to recover and adapt in the face of adversity, trauma, or serious stress. It isn't about avoiding life's challenges, but rather about developing the skills, emotional strength, and coping mechanisms needed to navigate them effectively. Resilient people are not immune to adversity, but they have the emotional tools and mental strength to face challenges, learn from them, and emerge stronger.

In today's unpredictable and rapidly changing world, building resilience is essential to maintaining mental health and well-being. Whether facing a personal challenge such as the loss of a loved one, a professional setback, or a global crisis, resilience enables people to meet setbacks with courage, adaptability, and emotional balance. In this chapter, we explore a range of strategies and tools for building resilience, including developing emotional intelligence, managing stress, reframing negative thinking, and building strong support networks. Understanding how to cultivate resilience can strengthen your ability to face life's inevitable challenges and help you build a fuller, more balanced life.

The Foundations of Resilience

Before diving into specific resilience-building strategies, it is important to understand the basic principles that underlie resilience. Resilience is built on several key pillars:

- **1. Emotional awareness:** Recognizing and understanding your emotions is essential to resilience. Emotional intelligence involves recognizing how emotions influence behaviour and using that awareness to guide thoughts and actions.

- **2. Adaptability:** The ability to adapt to new situations and challenges is essential to resilience. People who can adapt are less likely to be overwhelmed by change.

- **3. Optimism:** Maintaining an optimistic outlook, even in difficult times, is an important part of resilience. Optimism doesn't mean ignoring problems, but rather believing that they can be overcome.

- **4. Self-compassion:** Treating yourself with kindness and understanding during difficult times helps ease feelings of guilt, shame, or self-criticism that arise from setbacks.

- **5. Strong social connections:** Building meaningful relationships with others provides a vital support network during difficult times, offering emotional, psychological, and sometimes practical help.

By developing these foundational elements, people can build a framework that fosters resilience and emotional strength in the face of adversity.

Developing Emotional Intelligence and Stress Management Techniques

1. The Role of Emotional Intelligence in Resilience

Emotional intelligence (EI) is the ability to recognize, understand, and manage one's own emotions, as well as the ability to recognize and influence the emotions of others. This skill is essential for resilience, as it helps people manage and respond to stressful situations in healthy, constructive ways. Emotional intelligence has four main components:

- **1. Self-awareness:** The ability to recognize and understand your own emotions.

- **2. Self-regulation:** The ability to effectively manage or modify one's emotions and impulses.

- **3. Social awareness:** The ability to empathize with and understand others' emotions.

- **4. Relationship management:** Building and maintaining healthy relationships through effective communication and empathy.

Improving emotional intelligence builds resilience by helping individuals manage stress more effectively, make thoughtful decisions in difficult moments, and foster positive social interactions.

2. Strategies to Improve Emotional Intelligence

- **Mindfulness:** Practicing mindfulness increases self-awareness and helps people become more in tune with their emotions. Mindfulness meditation, in particular, encourages non-judgmental observation of thoughts and feelings, helping people recognize emotional patterns and respond to them calmly.

- **Active listening:** Paying close attention to others' emotions and responding with empathy strengthens relationships and increases social awareness.

- **Emotion regulation techniques:** Learning to self-regulate emotions like anger, frustration, and anxiety can prevent impulsive reactions and encourage more thoughtful responses. Techniques such as deep breathing, cognitive restructuring, and pausing before reacting can be effective in managing emotions.

3. Stress Management Techniques That Build Resilience

Stress is an inevitable part of life, but resilient people develop effective stress management strategies that allow them to handle pressure without becoming overwhelmed. Proven stress management techniques include:

- **Deep breathing and progressive muscle relaxation:** Controlled breathing techniques can reduce the body's stress response by slowing the heart rate and promoting relaxation. Progressive muscle relaxation (PMR) involves tensing and then relaxing various muscle groups to release physical tension associated with stress.

- **Physical activity:** Regular exercise is one of the most effective ways to reduce stress and improve mood. Exercise releases endorphins, which act as natural painkillers and help return the body to a calmer state after a stressful situation.

- **Time management and prioritization:** Learning how to effectively manage your time, prioritize tasks, and set realistic goals can reduce feelings of overwhelm. Breaking tasks into smaller, more manageable steps can help reduce stress related to work, school, or personal responsibilities.

- **Creative outlets:** Engaging in creative activities like writing, painting, or playing an instrument can reduce stress by providing emotional release and a healthy distraction from stressful situations.

By improving emotional intelligence and learning how to effectively manage stress, people can become more resilient and maintain emotional balance, even when facing significant challenges.

Cognitive Reframing and Managing Negative Thoughts

1. The Power of Cognitive Reframing

Cognitive reframing, or cognitive restructuring, is a psychological technique that involves changing the way we perceive and interpret negative or challenging situations. It is a powerful tool for resilience because it helps individuals shift their perspective, enabling them to view adversity in a more constructive and empowering light.

Negative thoughts and beliefs, often called cognitive distortions, can fuel feelings of helplessness, anxiety, and depression. Common cognitive distortions include:

- **Catastrophizing:** Anticipating the worst possible outcome or viewing a situation as far worse than it actually is.

- **Black-and-white thinking:** Seeing situations in extremes, with no middle ground (for example, framing everything as success or failure, good or bad).

- **Overgeneralization:** Drawing broad, negative conclusions from a single event.

- **Personalization:** Blaming yourself for events that are beyond your control.

Cognitive reframing involves challenging these distortions and replacing them with more balanced, realistic thoughts.

2. Steps for Cognitive Reframing

- **Identify negative thoughts:** The first step in cognitive reframing is becoming aware of negative thoughts and cognitive distortions as they arise. This requires self-awareness and mindfulness, since these thoughts often occur automatically.

- **Challenge negative beliefs:** Once you identify a negative belief, examine the evidence for and against it. Ask yourself questions like, "Is this really true?" or "Am I jumping to a conclusion?"

- **Replace negative thoughts:** After challenging a negative belief, replace it with a more balanced or realistic one. For example, instead of thinking "I always fail," try "I sometimes struggle, but I succeed in many areas of my life."

- **Practice gratitude:** Focusing on what is going well, rather than solely on what needs correcting, can shift your outlook toward a more positive and stable perspective.

3. Managing Negative Thoughts and Building Optimism

While negative thoughts are a natural part of the human experience, resilient individuals learn to manage them effectively. Strategies for managing negative thoughts include:

- **Journaling:** Writing down negative thoughts can help bring them to the surface and allow you to examine them more objectively. Journaling also provides an opportunity to reflect on positive experiences and accomplishments.

- **Positive affirmations:** Repeating positive, self-affirming statements can counteract negative thoughts and reinforce a more optimistic outlook.

- **Visualization:** Visualization techniques involve imagining a positive outcome or a peaceful scenario. This can help reduce anxiety and stress, especially when facing difficult situations.

Cultivating optimism doesn't mean ignoring problems — it means holding onto the belief that problems can be solved and positive outcomes are possible. Resilient people often focus on their strengths and coping skills, which helps them maintain hope even in difficult circumstances.

Building a Support Network and Strengthening Meaningful Connections

1. The Importance of Social Support in Building Resilience

Humans are inherently social, and building meaningful connections with others is one of the most effective ways to develop resilience. Social support can take many forms, including emotional support, practical help, and validation. Having a strong network of friends, family, and colleagues provides comfort during difficult times, helping people feel less isolated and better equipped to cope with life's challenges.

2. Types of Social Support

- **Emotional support:** This type of support includes empathy, understanding, and encouragement from others. Emotional support can help reduce feelings of loneliness, anxiety, or sadness and provide comfort during difficult times.

- **Informational support:** This involves receiving advice, guidance, or information that helps people make decisions or solve problems.

- **Instrumental support:** Practical help, such as assistance with tasks, financial support, or housing assistance, is known as instrumental support. This type of support can relieve immediate stress and allow people to focus on their emotional recovery.

3. Building and Strengthening Your Support Network

Building a strong support network takes effort and dedication. Here are some ways to foster and strengthen your social connections:

- **Maintain open communication:** Being honest and open about your feelings and experiences leads to deeper connections. Don't be afraid to ask for help when you need it.

- **Maintain relationships:** Invest time and energy in maintaining relationships with friends, family, and colleagues. Whether in person, on the phone, or online, regular communication helps strengthen bonds.

- **Seek out new connections:** Joining groups or communities that share common interests or goals is a great way to meet new people and build a support network. Consider joining a sports team, book club, or volunteer organization.

- **Be a supportive friend:** Offering support to others during their tough times helps create a reciprocal relationship of trust and care. When you show up for others, they are more likely to show up for you when you need them.

A strong support network provides not only emotional comfort but also practical solutions and advice to help people navigate difficulties effectively.

Setting Boundaries and Practicing Self-Compassion

1. The Role of Boundaries in Resilience

Setting healthy boundaries is essential for emotional well-being and resilience. Boundaries define what is acceptable in relationships and interactions, helping people protect their time, energy, and emotional resources. Without clear boundaries, people can feel overwhelmed, exhausted, and taken advantage of, which can weaken their resilience.

Boundaries aren't about distancing yourself from others, but about ensuring relationships remain balanced, respectful, and healthy.

2. Tips for Setting Healthy Boundaries

- **Know your limits:** Self-awareness is key to setting boundaries. Know what you can and can't tolerate, and be clear about your emotional and physical limits.

- **Communicate clearly:** When setting boundaries, communicate your needs clearly and assertively. Express your feelings using "I" statements, without blaming or criticizing the other person.

- **Practice saying no:** It's important to say no, when necessary, without feeling guilty or obligated to explain yourself. Saying no allows you to prioritize your well-being.

- **Respect other people's boundaries:** Just as you expect others to respect yours, it is important to respect the boundaries that others set.

3. Practicing Self-Compassion

Self-compassion involves treating yourself with the same kindness, care, and understanding you would show a friend. It's an important part of resilience because it helps people bounce back from setbacks without being overly critical or harsh on themselves.

Self-compassion consists of three elements:

- **Self-kindness:** Treating oneself with warmth and care, rather than with harsh judgment or criticism.

- **Common humanity:** Recognizing that suffering and failure are part of the shared human experience.

- **Mindfulness:** Acknowledging your emotions and experiences without getting caught up in or over-identifying with negative emotions.

Practicing self-compassion helps people build emotional resilience and maintain a positive, balanced attitude even during difficult times.

Conclusion: Building a Resilient Lifestyle

Building resilience is a lifelong process that involves growing emotional intelligence, developing healthy coping strategies, and nurturing meaningful connections. Learning how to manage stress, reframe negative thoughts, and set healthy boundaries can help people face life's challenges with more strength and confidence. Resilience isn't about avoiding adversity — it's about thriving in the face of it. With the right tools, mindset, and support, anyone can develop the emotional strength needed to weather life's ups and downs and emerge stronger from difficult challenges.

Chapter 7

Social Media, Technology, and Mental Health

Introduction

In the 21st century, technology has become an essential part of everyday life. Social media platforms connect billions of people around the world, offering endless opportunities for communication, entertainment, learning, and self-expression. These technological advances have brought many benefits, but they have also created new challenges, especially when it comes to mental health.

Social media platforms in particular have transformed the way people interact, perceive themselves, and engage with the world. While these platforms can foster connection and community, they can also contribute to anxiety, low self-esteem, and other mental health issues. Additionally, constant access to technology has led to a sense of digital overload, creating pressure to always be "on" and connected. This chapter examines the impact of social media and technology on mental health, providing readers with insight into how digital life can have both positive and negative effects on well-being. It examines how social media affects self-esteem, discusses the concept of digital detox, suggests strategies for creating a healthier online environment, and highlights the importance of genuine connection in the digital age.

The Influence of Social Media on Self-Esteem and Anxiety

1. The Growth of Social Media and Its Role in Modern Life

Social media platforms such as Instagram, Facebook, Twitter (X), TikTok, and Snapchat have changed how people communicate, share, and consume content. These platforms allow users to post photos, videos, thoughts, and experiences in real time, creating a highly interactive and visual environment. Social media is a valuable tool for staying connected with friends, family, and world events, but it can also have both positive and negative effects on users' mental health. Part of its appeal lies in its ability to present curated, often idealized versions of life. However, this highly curated nature can lead to comparison, unrealistic expectations, and feelings of inadequacy, especially when people compare their own lives to the seemingly perfect lives of others.

2. Social Comparison and Its Impact on Self-Esteem

One of the most significant ways social media can impact mental health is through social comparison. Social comparison theory suggests that individuals evaluate themselves by comparing their lives, achievements, and experiences to those of others. On social media, users are constantly exposed to the highlights of other people's lives — vacations, celebrations, accomplishments — which can create a distorted perception of reality. When we only see other people's best moments, we can begin to feel like our own lives are incomplete.

This constant comparison can lead to the following consequences:

- **Low self-esteem:** When people measure their self-worth against the edited, filtered, and often unrealistic version of reality presented on social media, they can feel inadequate. This can negatively impact self-esteem, especially among young people and those prone to anxiety.

- **Increased anxiety:** social media can heighten feelings of anxiety, especially when people feel pressure to follow trends, maintain a certain image, or gain approval through likes and comments. Fear of missing out (FOMO) and the pressure to present a perfect image can contribute to social anxiety and feelings of inadequacy.

3. The Role of Validation and Dopamine in Social Media Use

Social media platforms are designed to be engaging and often tap into the brain's reward system by offering instant gratification. Receiving likes, comments, and shares on a post can trigger the release of dopamine, a neurotransmitter associated with pleasure and reward. This creates a feedback loop in which users seek out more validation through social media interactions, leading to increased time spent on these platforms.

While this temporary dopamine boost may feel satisfying in the short term, it can create a dependency on external validation for self-worth. Over time, people may come to rely on social media approval to feel good about themselves, and a lack of approval can damage their inner self-esteem and lead to emotional instability.

4. Anxiety, FOMO, and the Pressure to Stay Connected

The pressure to stay constantly connected and informed on social media can contribute to anxiety and stress. Fear of missing out, commonly known as FOMO, is especially prevalent in the age of social media. FOMO refers to the anxiety or unease that arises from the belief that others are experiencing more fun, excitement, or fulfilment than oneself. Social media exacerbates FOMO by providing a continuous stream of updates, photos, and events that users may feel they are missing out on. FOMO can manifest in the following ways:

- **Increased anxiety:** Individuals may feel they need to check their social media accounts frequently, fearing they will miss important updates or opportunities. This can create a sense of urgency and stress.

- **Difficulty disconnecting:** The pressure to stay connected and up to date can make it difficult for individuals to take breaks from social media or fully enjoy real-life experiences without feeling the need to document them online.

While social media offers opportunities for connection and engagement, it is important to recognize the potential negative effects it can have on mental health. Recognizing these issues is the first step to building healthier online habits.

Digital Detox: Reducing Screen Time and Building Healthier Habits

1. The Concept of Digital Overload

As technology advances, so does the amount of time people spend on digital devices. The term "digital overload" refers to the feeling of being overwhelmed that results from excessive exposure to digital content, notifications, and constant connectivity. With the average person spending hours looking at a screen every day — whether for work, entertainment, or socializing — digital overload can have a negative impact on both mental and physical health.

Signs of digital overload include:

- **Mental fatigue:** Constantly switching between apps, platforms, and notifications can lead to cognitive overload and reduced focus.

- **Eye strain:** Prolonged screen time can cause digital eye strain, leading to headaches, blurred vision, and discomfort.

- **Sleep disturbances:** Excessive use of digital devices before bed, in particular, can disrupt sleep habits by interfering with melatonin production and the hormones that regulate sleep.

- **Increased stress and anxiety:** Constant exposure to digital content, including news, social media, and email, can contribute to feelings of stress and anxiety.

2. Benefits of a Digital Detox

A digital detox involves taking an intentional break from digital devices and social media to reduce mental clutter, ease stress, and restore balance. By stepping away from screens, people can reconnect with themselves, engage in real-world activities, and regain a sense of control over their digital habits. Some benefits of a digital detox include:

- **Improved mental clarity:** Avoiding constant notifications and digital distractions improves focus, reduces stress, and increases mental clarity.

- **Improved sleep quality:** Reducing screen time, especially before bed, helps improve sleep quality by allowing the brain to naturally calm down.

- **Improved mood:** Taking a break from social media and technology can reduce anxiety, comparison, and feelings of overwhelm, helping people feel more positive and balanced.

- **Improved productivity:** Without constant distractions from notifications and digital interruptions, people can be more productive and complete tasks more efficiently.

3. Strategies for Implementing a Digital Detox

While it's not realistic for most people to eliminate digital devices from their daily lives entirely, there are ways to reduce screen time and adopt healthier habits:

- **Set screen time limits:** Many smartphones and apps have screen time trackers that allow you to set daily limits for social media and other apps. Being aware of the time spent in front of screens can help people set limits and prioritize other activities.

- **Designate technology-free times and spaces:** Designating certain times of day (such as mealtimes or before bed) or areas of the home (such as the bedroom) as technology-free zones can help reduce digital overload and increase presence in daily life.

- **Engage in offline activities:** Rediscover hobbies and activities that don't involve screens, like reading a book, going for a walk, or practicing a creative skill. These offline activities provide a mental break and allow for more meaningful interaction with the world.

- **Practice mindfulness:** Incorporating mindfulness techniques such as meditation and deep breathing into everyday life can help people become more aware of their digital habits and make informed choices about how they use technology in the moment.

A digital detox doesn't have to be an all-or-nothing approach. Even small changes to daily habits can considerably reduce digital overload and improve mental well-being.

Cultivating a Positive Digital Environment

1. Taking Control of Your Online Experience

While the digital world can feel overwhelming at times, individuals have the power to shape and curate their online experiences in ways that promote positivity and well-being. A positive digital environment is one that fosters meaningful connection, inspires creativity, and supports mental health rather than compromising it.

2. Steps to Curate a Healthier Online Space

- **Unfollow or mute negative content:** Social media algorithms are designed to surface content based on user interactions. If certain accounts, pages, or groups consistently leave you feeling anxious, annoyed, or unsatisfied, consider unfollowing, muting, or blocking them. Surrounding yourself with positive, uplifting content improves your overall online experience.

- **Follow accounts that inspire and support you:** Look for accounts that promote mental health awareness, self-care, positivity, and creativity. Engaging with content that aligns with your values and interests can help you feel connected and motivated.

- **Be intentional about your content consumption:** With the endless scroll of social media, it's easy to lose track of time, so be deliberate about what you consume. Prioritize quality over quantity — content that adds value to your life rather than content that simply fills time.

- **Limit exposure to news and media:** While staying informed is important, excessive exposure to news, particularly negative news, can contribute to stress and anxiety. Consider limiting your news intake to specific times of day and to trusted, reliable sources.

- **Engage in meaningful interactions:** Instead of passively scrolling through social media, engage with others by commenting on and sharing posts that resonate with you. Making meaningful connections online strengthens your sense of community and belonging.

The Importance of Real Connection in a Digital Age

1. Balancing Online and Offline Relationships

While social media and technology provide opportunities for connection, they cannot fully replace the depth and richness of face-to-face relationships. Real-life connections — whether with family, friends, or community members — are essential for emotional support, personal growth, and overall well-being. Research shows that strong social connections are associated with better mental health, including lower levels of depression and anxiety, increased well-being, and greater resilience. In contrast, loneliness and social isolation can negatively impact mental health, contributing to sadness, anxiety, and feelings of alienation.

2. The Benefits of Personal Interaction

Personal interactions have several unique benefits that cannot be fully replicated through digital communication:

- **Non-verbal cues:** Face-to-face communication allows for the exchange of non-verbal cues such as facial expressions, body language, and tone of voice, which improve understanding and empathy.

- **Emotional connection:** Physical presence and shared experiences create a deeper emotional connection that fosters trust, intimacy, and support.

- **Reduced misunderstandings:** Digital communication can lead to misunderstandings due to a lack of context and non-verbal cues. In-person conversations allow for immediate clarification and conflict resolution.

3. Building and Nurturing Offline Relationships

While technology can complement human relationships, it's important to prioritize real-life connections to maintain emotional well-being. Here are some tips for building and nurturing offline relationships:

- **Make time for in-person interactions:** Schedule regular time to meet up in person with friends, family, and colleagues, whether that's for coffee, a walk, or a meal. These interactions provide opportunities for meaningful conversation and connection.

- **Participate in shared activities:** Participating in shared activities like hobbies, sports, and volunteer work strengthens bonds with others and creates lasting memories.

- **Practice active listening:** When interacting with others in person, practice active listening by giving them your full attention, making eye contact, and responding thoughtfully. This promotes deeper understanding and connection.

Conclusion: Finding Balance in the Digital Age

Social media and technology have undoubtedly transformed the way people live, work, and communicate. While our digital lives offer countless opportunities for connection and self-expression, they also pose unique challenges for our mental health. The key to maintaining emotional well-being in the digital age is balance.

By becoming aware of the impact social media and technology have on mental health, individuals can take proactive steps to manage their online habits, reduce digital overload, and foster positive, meaningful connections both online and offline. Whether through a digital detox, creating a healthier online environment, or prioritizing real-life relationships, these strategies allow people to navigate the digital landscape with greater awareness and control. Ultimately, technology is a tool that can improve or worsen well-being depending on how it's used. By making conscious choices and setting healthy boundaries, individuals can enjoy the benefits of the digital world while protecting their mental health and maintaining balance in their lives.

Chapter 8
The Journey of Healing — Embracing Growth and Change

Introduction

Recovery from mental health issues is a journey, not a destination. It is a process of self-discovery, growth, and transformation that takes time, patience, and continued effort. For many people, healing involves releasing past wounds, developing healthy coping strategies, and embracing change. Healing also means recognizing that it is not linear — there will be setbacks, breakthroughs, and everything in between. But every step forward is a victory worth celebrating, and overcoming each challenge helps build stronger self-esteem.

This chapter focuses on different aspects of healing and emphasizes the importance of perseverance, self-acceptance, and personal growth. We will explore the process of letting go of past trauma, the role of ongoing self-care, and how to maintain good mental health over the long term. Viewing healing as an ongoing journey rather than a fixed endpoint allows individuals to embrace the changes that come with growth and celebrate the progress made along the way.

The Healing Process: Patience, Self-Acceptance, and Growth

1. Healing Is a Non-Linear Journey

The road to recovery from mental health issues is never an easy one. Unlike physical injuries, which often follow a predictable healing process, emotional and psychological healing can be more complex. It involves facing deep-rooted emotions, working through unresolved trauma, and breaking unhealthy patterns of thinking and behaviour. It is important to recognize that this process takes time and that setbacks are a natural part of the journey.

Many people struggling with mental health challenges may feel discouraged when they don't see immediate improvement, or when old emotions resurface during the healing process. However, a setback doesn't mean failure — it's an opportunity to learn and grow. Every experience, whether positive or negative, contributes to personal development and builds resilience. Healing requires patience, not just with the process itself, but with yourself. Often the hardest part of healing is learning to forgive yourself for past mistakes, embrace imperfection, and accept that growth is an ongoing, ever-changing process.

2. Self-Acceptance: The Foundation of Healing

A key component of healing is self-acceptance. It involves recognizing and accepting all aspects of ourselves — strengths and weaknesses, successes and failures, joys and pain. Many people who struggle with mental health issues feel shame or guilt about their experiences. They may think of themselves as "broken" or "flawed" because of their struggles.

But self-acceptance means letting go of these judgments and accepting that everyone faces challenges in life. Mental health issues are not a reflection of a person's worth or character; they are simply part of the human experience. Practicing self-compassion is an important part of self-acceptance — it means treating yourself with kindness and understanding, especially during difficult times. Instead of engaging in self-criticism, people can learn to speak to themselves with the same kindness and empathy they would offer a close friend.

- **Acknowledge your feelings:** Healing begins with recognizing and accepting your feelings, rather than suppressing or denying them. It's normal to feel sad, angry, frustrated, or scared — these emotions are a natural part of the healing process.

- **Accept your imperfections:** No one is perfect, and expecting perfection can hinder healing. By allowing themselves room to grow and recognizing that growth comes through practice, people can release unrealistic expectations and develop healthier self-perceptions.

- **Practice forgiveness:** Healing often involves letting go of past guilt and regret. Self-forgiveness is a powerful tool that allows a person to move forward without being held back by past mistakes.

3. Growth Through Healing

Healing from mental health issues often leads to significant personal growth. This growth can take the form of increased self-awareness, emotional intelligence, and resilience. The healing process allows individuals to develop new perspectives, gain insight into their emotions and behaviours, and cultivate healthier ways of thinking and responding to life's challenges.

Growth through healing may involve:

- **Increased self-awareness:** Healing requires introspection and self-reflection. By examining their thoughts, feelings, and behaviours, individuals can gain a deeper understanding of themselves and their triggers.

- **Building emotional intelligence:** As people focus on healing, they develop greater emotional intelligence — the ability to understand and manage their emotions effectively. This skill is essential for maintaining healthy relationships and coping with stress.

- **Developing resilience:** Overcoming mental health challenges builds resilience, or the ability to bounce back from adversity. The obstacles faced and setbacks overcome strengthen an individual's capacity to handle future challenges.

Ultimately, the journey of healing is a journey of self-discovery. It allows individuals to uncover their inner strength, build new coping mechanisms, and grow into the best version of themselves.

Accepting Change and Letting Go of Past Trauma

1. The Importance of Letting Go

One of the most difficult aspects of healing is learning to let go of past trauma. Trauma — whether the result of a childhood experience, a relationship, or any other life event — can leave deep emotional scars and affect a person's mental health and well-being for years, or even decades, after the event itself occurred. Healing from trauma involves acknowledging its impact, processing the emotions associated with it, and ultimately releasing its hold on your life. Letting go does not mean forgetting or erasing the past. Instead, it means accepting that traumatic events shaped your experience without allowing them to define your future. Letting go is about reclaiming your strength and freeing yourself from cycles of pain, guilt, or anger that can otherwise leave lasting wounds.

2. The Role of Therapy in Healing

Healing from trauma often requires specialized support, such as therapy. Trauma-focused treatments, including cognitive behavioural therapy (CBT), Eye Movement Desensitization and Reprocessing (EMDR), and dialectical behaviour therapy (DBT), are specifically designed to support healing from trauma. Therapy provides a safe and supportive space for people to explore their trauma, identify patterns of behaviour that may have developed as coping mechanisms, and learn new strategies for managing distress. Through therapy, people can gradually come to terms with their past, release pent-up emotions, and find a sense of closure.

3. Accepting Change as Part of Healing

Healing and personal growth require accepting change. Change can be difficult, especially when it requires altering long-held beliefs, behaviours, or thought patterns, but it is an essential part of the healing process. As people recover, they may find that their perspective shifts, their relationships evolve, and their priorities change. This can be both exciting and unsettling. It is important to approach change with an open mind and a willingness to adapt. By embracing change, people can continue to grow and develop, creating a life that is more aligned with their values and goals.

Key strategies for embracing change include:

- **Practicing mindfulness:** Mindfulness helps individuals stay present and accept change as it occurs. Focusing on the present moment can help people feel less anxious about the future and develop greater resilience in the face of uncertainty.

- **Focusing on growth:** Try viewing change as an opportunity for growth rather than something to fear. Change often opens new doors and creates opportunities for personal development.

- **Developing flexibility:** Being flexible in your thinking and approach to life makes it easier to navigate change. With flexibility, people can adapt to new situations and embrace the unknown.

Healing requires a shift in perspective — from resisting change to accepting it as a natural and necessary part of life. When people approach change with openness and curiosity, it creates space for healing and transformation.

The Importance of Continuing Self-Care and Maintaining Mental Health

1. Healing as a Continuing Process

One of the most important realizations on the road to recovery is that self-care and maintaining mental health are ongoing practices. Healing has no true endpoint — it is a continuous process of nurturing mental, emotional, and physical well-being. Mental health requires consistent care and attention, just as physical health requires regular exercise, healthy nutrition, and rest.

Self-care is not a one-time fix; it is a lifelong commitment to yourself. It involves identifying your needs, setting healthy boundaries, and engaging in activities that promote well-being. Self-care practices can include physical activities like exercise, mental activities like meditation or journaling, and emotional activities like connecting with loved ones or engaging in creative pursuits.

2. Developing a Self-Care Routine

Creating a self-care routine is important for maintaining long-term mental health. A well-rounded routine should address various aspects of well-being, including physical, emotional, and mental health. Here are some key elements of a balanced self-care routine:

- **Physical health:** Regular exercise, sufficient sleep, and a nutritious diet are essential for both physical and mental health. Engaging in physical activity like walking, yoga, or swimming can reduce stress and improve mood.

- **Emotional health:** Emotional self-care involves acknowledging and expressing your emotions in healthy ways. This might include talking to a close friend, writing in a journal, or participating in therapy.

- **Mental health:** Mental self-care includes activities that promote cognitive health, such as practicing mindfulness, setting realistic goals, and challenging negative thought patterns.

- **Social connections:** Maintaining healthy relationships and participating in social activities are important aspects of self-care. Surrounding yourself with supportive, positive people can provide emotional nourishment and reduce feelings of loneliness or isolation.

- **Creative expression:** Engaging in creative activities such as painting, writing, or music can provide an emotional outlet and promote a sense of fulfilment and purpose.

3. Recognizing the Need for Extra Support

Even when you are taking good care of yourself, you may still need extra support. Mental health is not static, and life's challenges can sometimes become overwhelming. It's important to recognize when self-help isn't enough and to seek professional help if needed. Seeking support through therapy, counselling, or support groups is a sign of strength, not weakness. It shows that you're committed to your health and are prioritizing your mental well-being.

Celebrating Progress and Personal Victories

1. Acknowledging Small Wins

Healing is a journey filled with both large and small milestones. It's important to recognize and celebrate each one. Whether it's getting through a tough day, challenging a negative thought, or setting a healthy boundary, every step forward is evidence of personal growth.

Celebrating small victories helps reinforce positive change and provides motivation to continue on the path to recovery. It also fosters a sense of accomplishment and self-esteem.

2. Reflecting on Growth

Taking time to reflect on personal growth is a powerful way to celebrate progress. Reflection allows people to see how far they've come, acknowledge the challenges they've overcome, and appreciate the strength and resilience they've developed along the way. Journaling can serve as a reflective tool: writing about one's experiences allows individuals to gain a deeper understanding of their emotional journey and track their growth over time.

3. Practicing Gratitude

Practicing gratitude is another powerful way to celebrate progress. Focusing on the positive aspects of life, even during challenging times, can shift one's mindset and promote a sense of peace and contentment. Gratitude can be practiced through journaling, meditation, or simply taking a few moments each day to reflect on what you're thankful for.

1. Acknowledging Small Wins

Conclusion: Embracing the Ongoing Healing Journey

The healing journey is a lifelong process that involves self-discovery, growth, and transformation. It requires patience, self-acceptance, and a willingness to embrace change. Recovery from mental health issues is not a linear path, but with each step forward — no matter how small — individuals can build resilience, develop emotional strength, and create a life that aligns with their values and goals. By focusing on self-care, celebrating progress, and seeking support when needed, individuals can walk the path to recovery with greater confidence and peace. Healing is progress, not perfection, and every step is a victory worth celebrating.